MARSHMALLOW PEOPLE

AND THE SUFFOCATING DESPAIR OF EXISTENCE

BY JASON STEELE

FOR SCUFFY

THANK YOU FOR MAKING THE SUFFOCATING
DESPAIR OF EXISTENCE SLIGHTLY LESS SUFFOCATING.

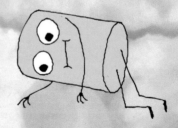

SPEAKING OF VIOLENCE, WE COULD TRY VIOLENCE.

LET'S FIND THE TRIANGLE PEOPLE AND VIOLENCE THEM. I'VE RARELY NOT CARED ABOUT VIOLENCE.

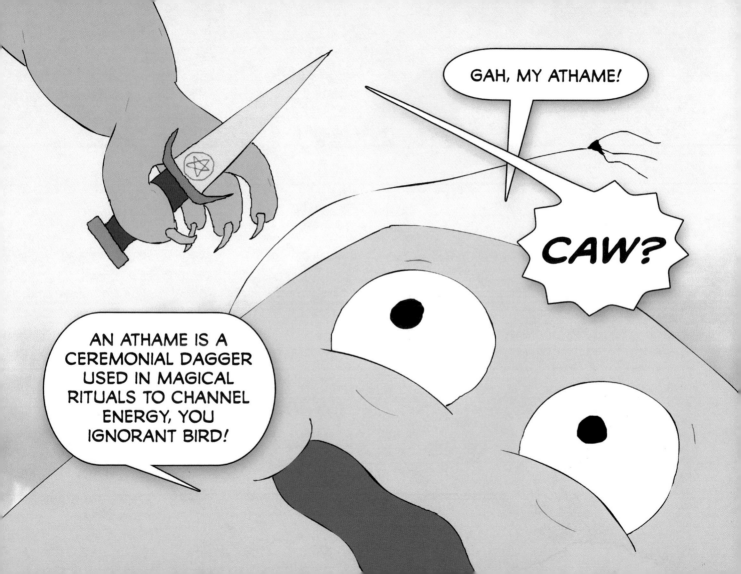

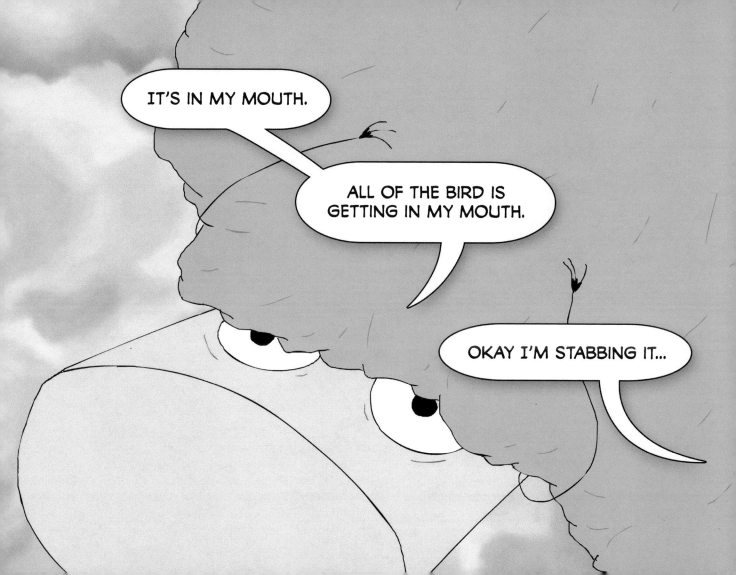

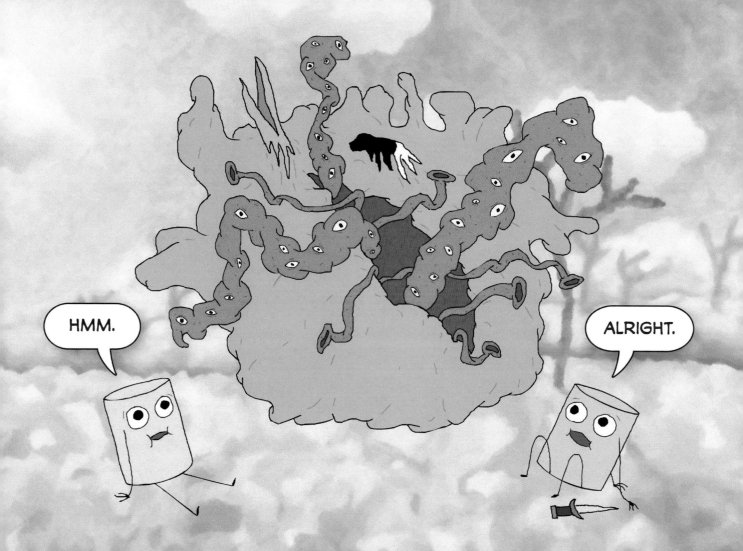

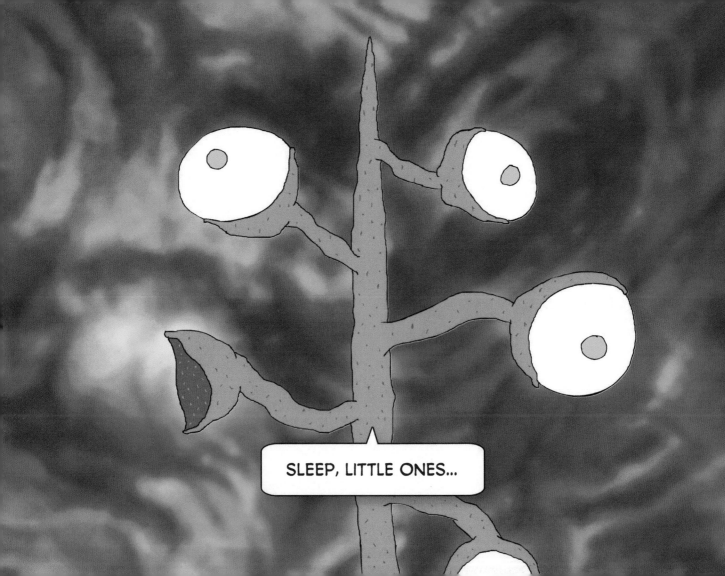

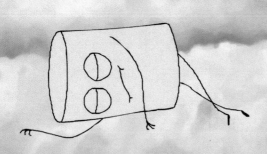

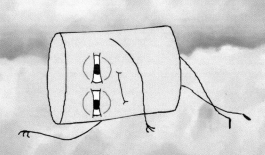

Made in the USA
Charleston, SC
05 December 2016